Easy-to-Make **Felt**

Ornaments

for Christmas and
other Occasions

With full-size templates

by Betty Deems

Dover Publications, Inc., New York

Published in Canada by General Publishing Company, Ltd., 30 Lesmill Road, Don Mills, Toronto, Ontario.
Published in the United Kingdom by Constable and Company, Ltd., 10 Orange Street, London WC 2.

This Dover edition, first published in 1976, is a new collection of ornaments from *Heirloom Ornaments*, published by Betty Deems in 1974 and *Heirloom Ornaments II*, published by Betty Deems in 1975. The instructions and templates have been prepared especially for this edition.
The publisher wishes to thank Carolyn M. De Angelis, Canandaigua, New York 14424 for permission to use the *Deer, Santa Claus, Mrs. Santa Claus, Red-Haired Roy* and *Red-Haired Robin.*

International Standard Book Number:
0-486-23389-8
Library of Congress Catalog Card Number:
76-18405

Manufactured in the United States of America
Dover Publications, Inc.
180 Varick Street
New York, N.Y. 10014

Introduction

This book contains full-size templates and step-by-step instructions for making 35 felt ornaments. They can be used to decorate your Christmas tree, as holiday house decorations, party favors, gifts or toys.

All of the component shapes used in the ornaments are given in actual-size templates printed on heavy paper. Locate the designated templates and carefully cut them out. To keep the edges of the cardboard as neat and firm as possible, use a large scissors, a single-edged razor blade or an X-acto knife. Since these templates are all reusable, make certain that you keep all of the templates together for a particular ornament. You might want to put them in a small envelope marked with the name of the ornament.

The special materials needed for each ornament are listed with the directions for making that item. In addition you will need cotton or polyester stuffing and a thick, clear-drying glue that is suitable for fabrics. When you have finished making your ornament, attach a loop for hanging. Clear fishing line makes an excellent and inexpensive loop which will be almost invisible. You can also use gold thread as a loop.

When sewing the ornaments together, start at the small hard-to-stuff places, stuffing as you sew. Push in the stuffing with the points of a small scissors or other thin, sharp object as you sew. Use small overcast stitches, and match thread to felt to make the stitches less visible.

If you are making a large number of ornaments, buy felt by the yard. If you are making less than four, buy felt by the square. Save all of your felt scraps for decorating other ornaments.

You can follow the instructions exactly as they are given, or add your own individual touches of facial expressions and trimmings to make your ornaments uniquely yours. For instance, I have used both plastic movable eyes and felt circles for the eyes. You can use either of these interchangeably, or you can embroider eyes and facial features or even draw them on with a felt-tip marking pen. Paper punches are very handy for cutting circles out of felt for eyes and cheeks.

You will enjoy making my easy-to-make felt ornaments, and your handmade ornaments, with your own special touches, will make your holiday occasion more beautiful and meaningful each year.

Goldfish

The template used to make this ornament appears on Plate 16.

MATERIALS

Bright yellow felt
Bright yellow thread
24 Gold sequins
2 Green sequins
Gold glitter

DIRECTIONS

1. Trace appropriate template on felt and cut out the pieces.
2. Sew the two body pieces together, stuffing as you sew.
3. On both sides, glue gold sequins, and green sequins for eyes.
4. Draw lines on fins and tail with glue and sprinkle lines with gold glitter. Shake off excess glitter.

Patsy Panda

The templates used to make this ornament appear on Plate 2.

MATERIALS

White, red, black and green felt
White thread

DIRECTIONS

1. Trace appropriate templates on felt and cut out the pieces.
2. Cut ears off front body piece only, and sew the two body pieces together, stuffing as you sew.
3. Glue black ear linings on ears.
4. Glue black paws and red heart on the body.
5. Sew face piece on head.
6. Cut two black circles for pupils and glue these on the green eyes. Glue eyes on face.
7. Cut a small red circle for the nose and glue on the face.
8. Draw a mouth with black ink.

Frog

The templates used to make this ornament appear on Plate 2.

MATERIALS

Green and red felt
Green thread
2 Green "jewels"
2 Large plastic eyes (or white and black felt)

DIRECTIONS

1. Trace appropriate templates on felt and cut out the pieces.
2. Fit the two body pieces together, sewing from A to B, to leave fingers free at the ends of the arms.
3. Sew the rest of the body pieces together, stuffing as you sew.
4. Put the vest on the frog, lapping over in front and gluing closing.
5. Glue on green "jewels" for buttons.
6. Cut out a red felt mouth and glue on frog.
7. Glue on plastic eyes, or cut two white circles and two smaller black ones and glue on for eyes.

Angel

The templates used to make this ornament appear on Plate 8.

MATERIALS

Pink, red and brown felt
Pink thread
Yellow fine yarn
¼" Blue velvet ribbon
Flower
Gold fringe
White glitter

DIRECTIONS

1. Trace appropriate templates on felt and cut out the pieces.
2. Beginning with hand, sew two body pieces together, stuffing as you sew.
3. Make hair by wrapping yarn around two fingers twelve times. Tie in the middle and cut through the loops at each end. Fan yarn out, and glue knot to the top of the head. Cut bangs in front and, if the hair is too long, trim the ends.
4. Sew the wings to the back, placing the fold on the seam line of the body.
5. Put velvet ribbon around the middle of the body and sew or glue in place. Glue flower on the ribbon.
6. Sew fringe around head for a crown, and glue on red felt mouth and brown felt eyelashes.
7. Brush glue on wings and sprinkle with white glitter.

Sammy Seal

The templates used to make this ornament appear on Plate 12.

MATERIALS

Black, white and red felt
Black and red thread
2 Plastic eyes

DIRECTIONS

1. Trace appropriate templates on felt and cut out the pieces.
2. Sew together the two body pieces, stuffing as you sew.
3. Sew together the two ball pieces, stuffing as you sew, and sew to the top of the head.
4. Glue on front piece and eyes.

Bunny

The templates used to make this ornament appear on Plate 16.

MATERIALS

White and pink felt
White thread
White chenille ball
Blue glitter tape (or blue felt)
2 Red sequins

DIRECTIONS

1. Trace appropriate templates on felt and cut out the pieces.
2. Sew two body pieces together, leaving ears free by stitching from A to B, and stuffing as you sew.
3. Glue ear linings inside ears.
4. Cut and glue pink felt on each side of nose. Cut two eyes from pink felt and glue on bunny. Glue a red sequin on pink eye.
5. Make a collar of blue glitter tape (or use blue felt) and glue on bunny.
6. Glue chenille ball to back of bunny for tail.

Eskimo

The templates used to make this ornament appear on Plate 3.

MATERIALS

White, black, light pink and deep pink felt
White thread
1 Large black sequin
2 Gold sequins
4 Red sequins
1 Small red bead
Gold double loop braid
Cream fringe
Gold cord
Gold cocktail pick

DIRECTIONS

1. Trace appropriate templates on felt and cut out the pieces.
2. Sew feet and hands between the two body pieces, and sew the two body pieces together, stuffing as you sew.
3. Sew face piece on front of head, and glue hair on face. Cut large black sequin in half and glue on face for eyebrows. With a paper punch, cut two deep pink felt circles and glue under eyebrows. Glue on red sequin mouth and small red bead nose.
4. Glue a strip of deep pink felt down the middle of the body front, and glue braid on the strip and the sleeves. Glue red sequins on sleeves and front braid, and glue gold sequins on feet.
5. Sew fringe around face and on bottom of the skirt. Glue gold cord tie on braid under chin.
6. Glue cocktail pick on hand and on braid. Fold the bottom of the hand over the "harpoon" and glue shut.

Jester

The templates used to make this ornament appear on Plate 7.

MATERIALS

Red and flesh-colored felt
Red and green thread
1 Ft. green velvet tubing
1 Pipe cleaner
5 Gold sequins
2 Black sequins
1 Red sequin
Off-white fine yarn
2 Bells
Gold cord
Gold braid

DIRECTIONS

1. Trace appropriate templates on felt and cut out the pieces.
2. Sew together the two head pieces, stuffing as you sew.
3. Sew face piece on front of head.
4. Sew loops of yarn behind hat piece at lower edge and trim for hair. Sew hat onto head.
5. Cut velvet tubing into two equal pieces. After pulling cord from one piece of tubing, run a pipe cleaner through the hollow tubing and sew under body piece at center of fold to make arms. Bend as in illustration and trim off all but ¼″ of the pipe cleaner at the end of each arm. Glue 2 hands together over the ends of the pipe cleaner, and glue a small piece of gold cord at the cuffs.
6. To make the legs, fold the other piece of tubing and sew at center to the same spot as you sewed the pipe cleaner arms. Sew bells on the ends of the legs.
7. Close body piece at bottom center point with a few stitches, and attach head to body as in illustration.
8. Glue gold braid and gold sequins on body and hat.
9. Glue black sequin eyes, red sequin nose and a red felt mouth on face.

Christmas Wreath

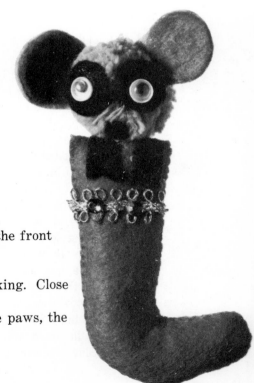

The templates used to make this ornament appear on Plate 11.

MATERIALS

Green and red felt
Green thread
Gold double loop braid
14 Small red sequins

DIRECTIONS

1. Trace appropriate templates on felt and cut out the pieces.
2. Sew the two wreath pieces together around the outer edge. Sew inner circle edges together, stuffing as you sew.
3. Sew gold braid around inner circle, and glue bow to wreath as illustrated.
4. Glue five red sequins, overlapping each other, on bow.
5. Glue three red sequins on wreath in three places as illustrated.

Mouse-in-a-Stocking

The templates used to make this ornament appear on Plate 6.

MATERIALS

Red, green and black felt
Red thread
2 Green chenille balls
Gold double loop braid
2 "Jewels"
2 Plastic eyes

DIRECTIONS

1. Trace appropriate templates on felt and cut out the pieces.
2. Glue two head pieces together, and glue a chenille ball on the front and the back of the head. Glue on red ear linings.
3. Sew stocking pieces together, leaving top open.
4. Stuff stocking, inserting neck of head into center of stocking. Close top of stocking with overcast stitches.
5. Cut a black felt circle for the nose, and glue the nose, the paws, the eyes, the gold braid and the "jewels" on the ornament.
6. Glue the tail on the *back* of the stocking.

10

Pony

The templates used to make this ornament appear on Plate 5.

MATERIALS

Green and red felt
Red thread
Gold double loop braid
2 Gold sequins

DIRECTIONS

1. Trace appropriate templates on felt and cut out the pieces.
2. Make a tail of four short strips of red felt and sew between the two body pieces at the back of the horse.
3. Sew the mane between the two body pieces on the head, leaving the ears free. Cut mane into strips.
4. Sew remainder of body pieces together, starting with eyes, stuffing as you sew, and pushing stuffing into legs with point of small scissors or other sharp object.
5. Glue gold braid on each side of saddle and glue saddle on body.
6. Cut six green felt petal-shaped pieces and glue on the head with a gold sequin in the center. Repeat for the other side of the head.

Reindeer Head

The templates used to make this ornament appear on Plate 13.

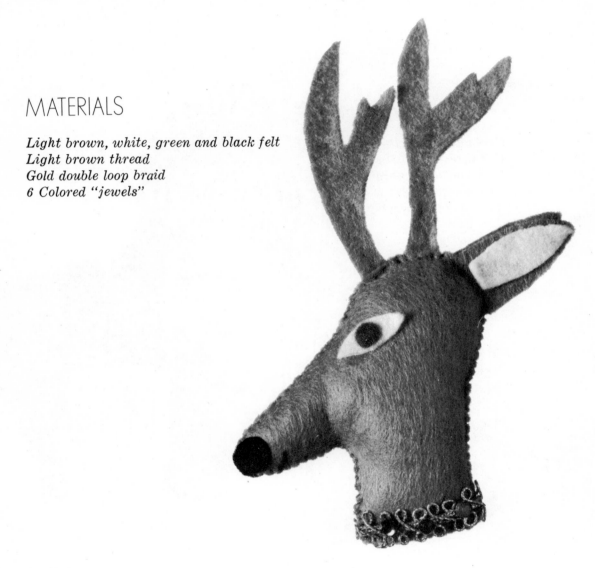

MATERIALS

Light brown, white, green and black felt
Light brown thread
Gold double loop braid
6 Colored "jewels"

DIRECTIONS

1. Trace the appropriate templates on felt and cut out the pieces.
2. Glue two antler pieces together for each antler, and sew between two head pieces on head.
3. Sew head pieces, leaving ears free by stitching from A to B, and stuffing as you sew.
4. Glue ear linings on each side.
5. Glue on black felt nose, white eyes and green pupils.
6. Glue braid around neck, and glue various colored "jewels" around collar.
7. Draw mouth with black ink.

Clown Head

The templates used to make this ornament appear on Plate 7.

MATERIALS

Pink, green and yellow felt
Pink and green thread
White chenille ball
2 Green spangle sequins
2 Large plastic eyes
Gold braid
Orange rug yarn
Flower

DIRECTIONS

1. Trace the appropriate templates on felt and cut out the pieces.
2. Sew head pieces together, stuffing as you sew.
3. Glue short pieces of rug yarn to each side of the head.
4. Glue on green spangle sequins, and glue plastic eyes on top of sequins. Glue on chenille ball and mouth. Draw a red mouth inside yellow mouth with pen.
5. Sew two hat pieces together, leaving bottom open. Stuff hat lightly; fit over head and stitch to head.
6. Glue gold braid to hat. Sew flower stem to hat.

Santa Claus

The templates used to make this ornament appear on Plate 13.

MATERIALS

*Red, white, black, light pink and
deep pink felt*
Red thread

DIRECTIONS

1. Trace the appropriate templates on felt and cut out the pieces.
2. Glue two boot pieces together for each boot, and sew between the two body sections.
3. Glue two mittens together for each mitten, and sew between the sleeves of the two body sections.
4. Sew the two body pieces together, stuffing as you sew.
5. Glue the face on the head. Position beard on face to determine where nose belongs. Remove beard, and glue nose in place. Glue beard and two black felt eyes on face.
6. Glue tassels on front and back of hat point.
7. Cut a strip of black felt for belt and glue on body. Glue buckle on belt.

Mrs. Santa Claus

The templates used to make this ornament appear on Plate 14.

MATERIALS

Red, white, pink, green, blue and black felt
Red thread
3 Small white sequins

DIRECTIONS

1. Trace the appropriate templates on felt and cut out the pieces.
2. Sew hand between the two body pieces. Glue two foot pieces together to make each foot, and sew the feet between the two body pieces.
3. Sew the body pieces together, stuffing as you sew, but do not stuff the neck.
4. Glue the neck between the face and the back of the hair. Let dry, and glue the front of the hair on the face.
5. Glue apron on the front of the body. Cut a red square and glue it on apron for a pocket. Glue three white sequins on the pocket.
6. Decorate the stocking with green leaves and red holly berry cut from felt, and glue stocking to hand.
7. Draw on spectacles, mouth and eyes with pen, or outline with embroidery thread.

Red Bird

The templates used to make this ornament appear on Plate 11.

MATERIALS

Red felt
Red thread
Red glitter
Green "jewels"

DIRECTIONS

1. Trace appropriate templates on felt and cut out the pieces.
2. Starting with beak, sew the body pieces together, stuffing as you sew.
3. Glue two wing pieces together for each wing, and sew on body.
4. Brush glue on both sides of beak and on tail, and sprinkle glitter on glue, shaking off excess.
5. Glue green "jewel" eyes on each side.

Deer

The templates used to make this ornament appear on Plate 6.

MATERIALS

Light brown, white, red and green felt
Light brown thread
4 Small red sequins

DIRECTIONS

1. Trace appropriate templates on felt and cut out the pieces.
2. Cut out the triangle between the legs on the body pieces and sew the two body pieces together around this opening.
3. Glue two antler pieces together for each antler and sew the antlers on the head between the two body pieces.
4. Starting with feet, sew the body pieces together, stuffing as you sew.
5. Glue nose on face, and draw eyes with black ink.
6. Cut two holly leaves from green felt and glue on front and back as shown, using small red sequins for berries.

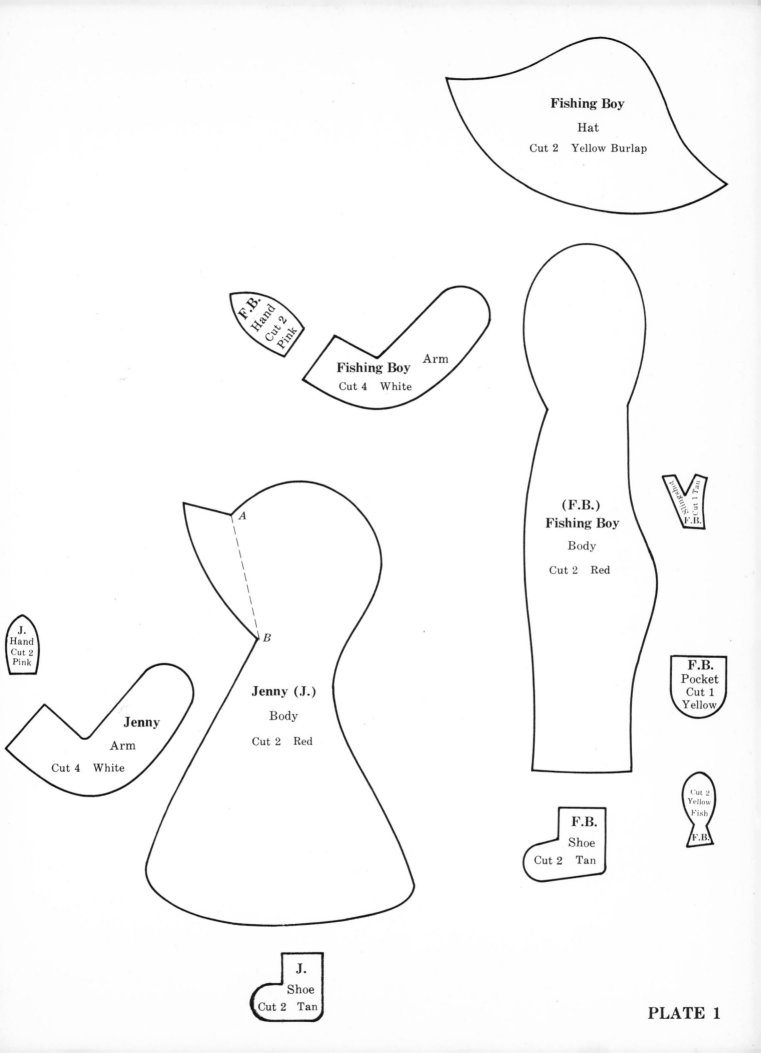

Fishing Boy

Hat

Cut 2   Yellow Burlap

F.B.
Hand
Cut 2
Pink

Fishing Boy   Arm

Cut 4   White

(F.B.)
Fishing Boy

Body

Cut 2   Red

Slingshot
Cut 1 Tan
F.B.

J.
Hand
Cut 2
Pink

Jenny

Arm

Cut 4   White

A

B

Jenny (J.)

Body

Cut 2   Red

F.B.
Pocket
Cut 1
Yellow

Cut 2
Yellow
Fish

F.B.

F.B.

Shoe

Cut 2   Tan

J.

Shoe

Cut 2   Tan

PLATE 1

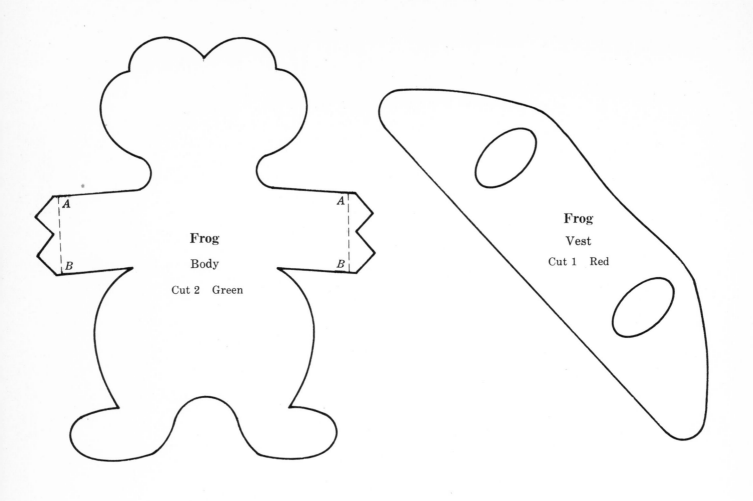

Frog

Body

Cut 2   Green

A

B

A

B

Frog

Vest

Cut 1   Red

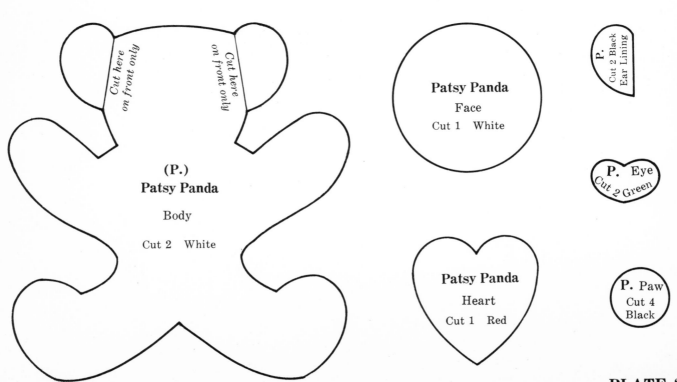

Cut here on front only

Cut here on front only

(P.)
Patsy Panda

Body

Cut 2   White

Patsy Panda

Face

Cut 1   White

P.
Cut 2 Black
Ear Lining

P.   Eye
Cut 2 Green

Patsy Panda

Heart

Cut 1   Red

P. Paw
Cut 4
Black

PLATE 2

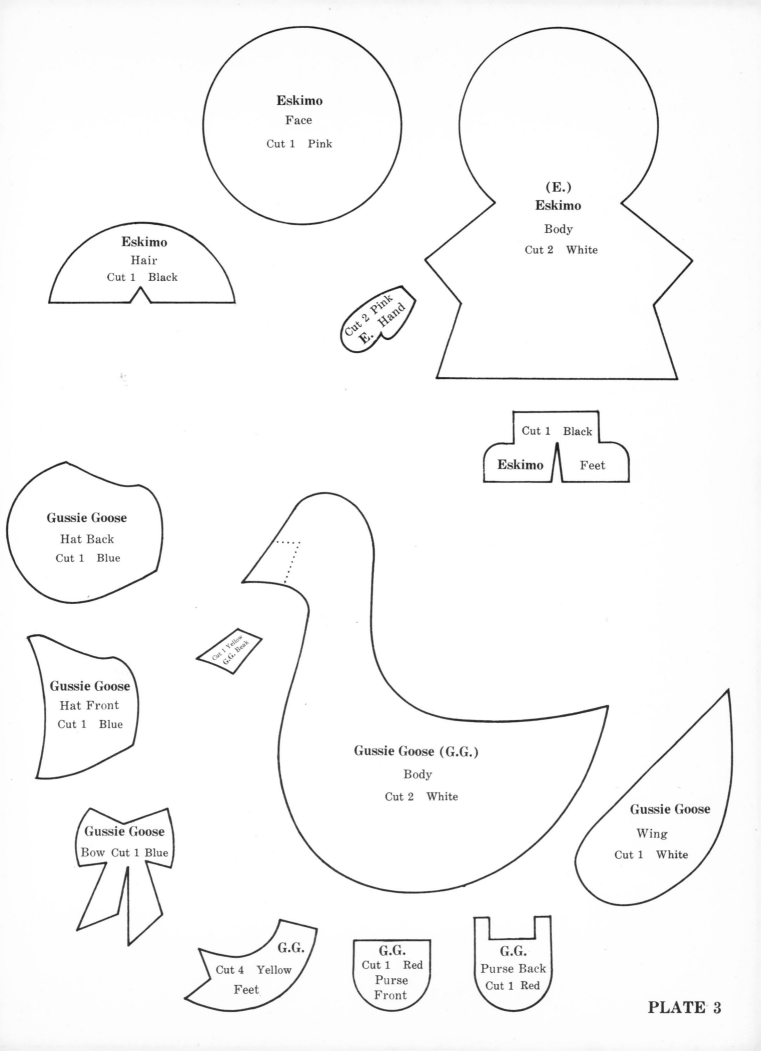

Eskimo

Face

Cut 1   Pink

(E.)
Eskimo

Body

Cut 2   White

Eskimo

Hair
Cut 1   Black

Cut 2 Pink
E. Hand

Cut 1   Black

Eskimo   Feet

Gussie Goose

Hat Back

Cut 1   Blue

Cut 1 Yellow
G.G. Beak

Gussie Goose

Hat Front

Cut 1   Blue

Gussie Goose (G.G.)

Body

Cut 2   White

Gussie Goose

Wing

Cut 1   White

Gussie Goose

Bow Cut 1 Blue

G.G.

Cut 4   Yellow

Feet

G.G.

Cut 1   Red

Purse

Front

G.G.

Purse Back

Cut 1   Red

PLATE 3

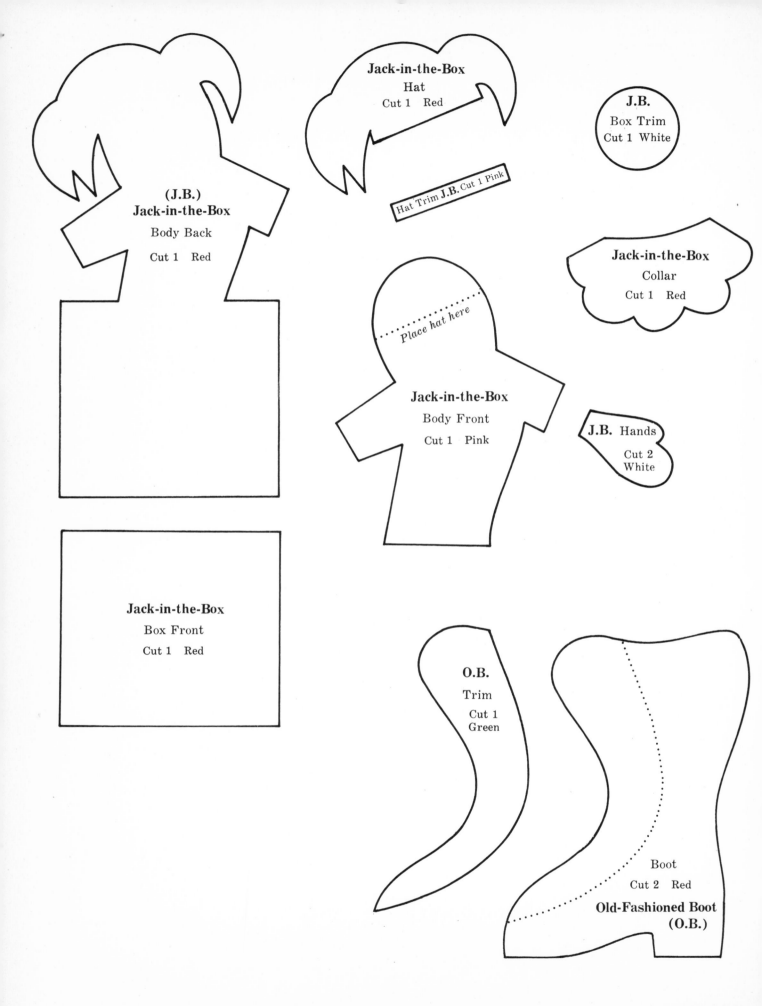

Jack-in-the-Box
Hat
Cut 1   Red

J.B.
Box Trim
Cut 1 White

Hat Trim **J.B.** Cut 1 Pink

(J.B.)
Jack-in-the-Box
Body Back
Cut 1   Red

Jack-in-the-Box
Collar
Cut 1   Red

Place hat here

Jack-in-the-Box
Body Front
Cut 1   Pink

J.B. Hands
Cut 2
White

Jack-in-the-Box
Box Front
Cut 1   Red

O.B.
Trim
Cut 1
Green

Boot
Cut 2   Red

Old-Fashioned Boot
(O.B.)

PLATE 4

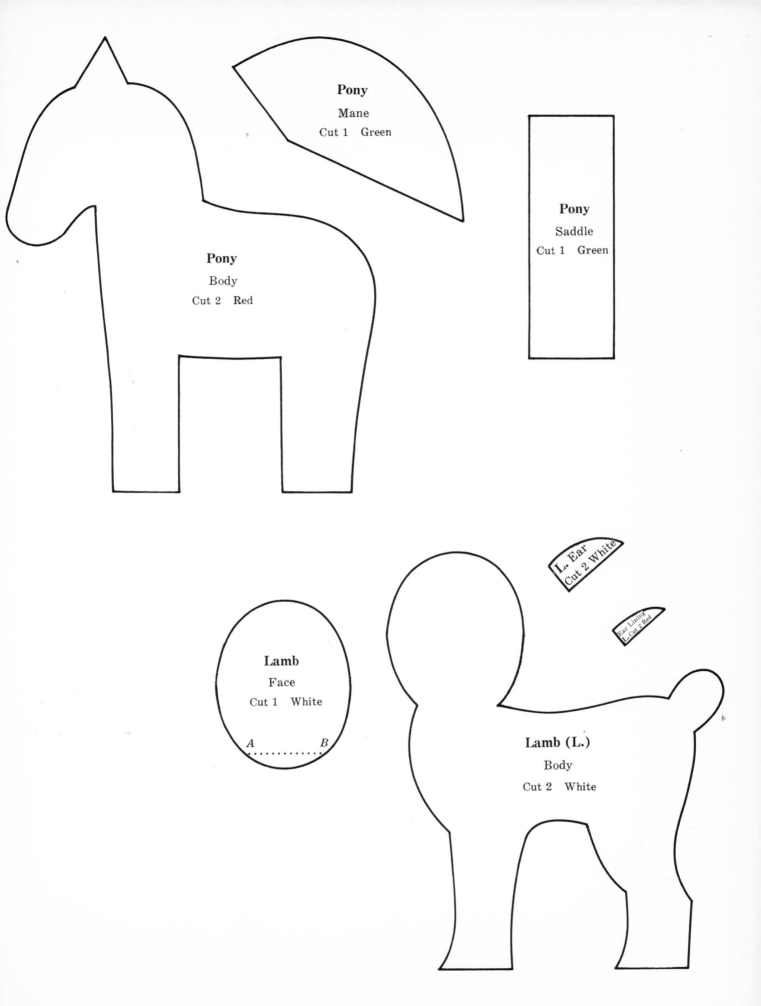

Pony

Mane

Cut 1   Green

Pony

Saddle

Cut 1   Green

Pony

Body

Cut 2   Red

Lamb

Face

Cut 1   White

A . . . . *B*

L. Ear
Cut 2 White

Ear Lining
L. Cut 2 Red

Lamb (L.)

Body

Cut 2   White

PLATE 5

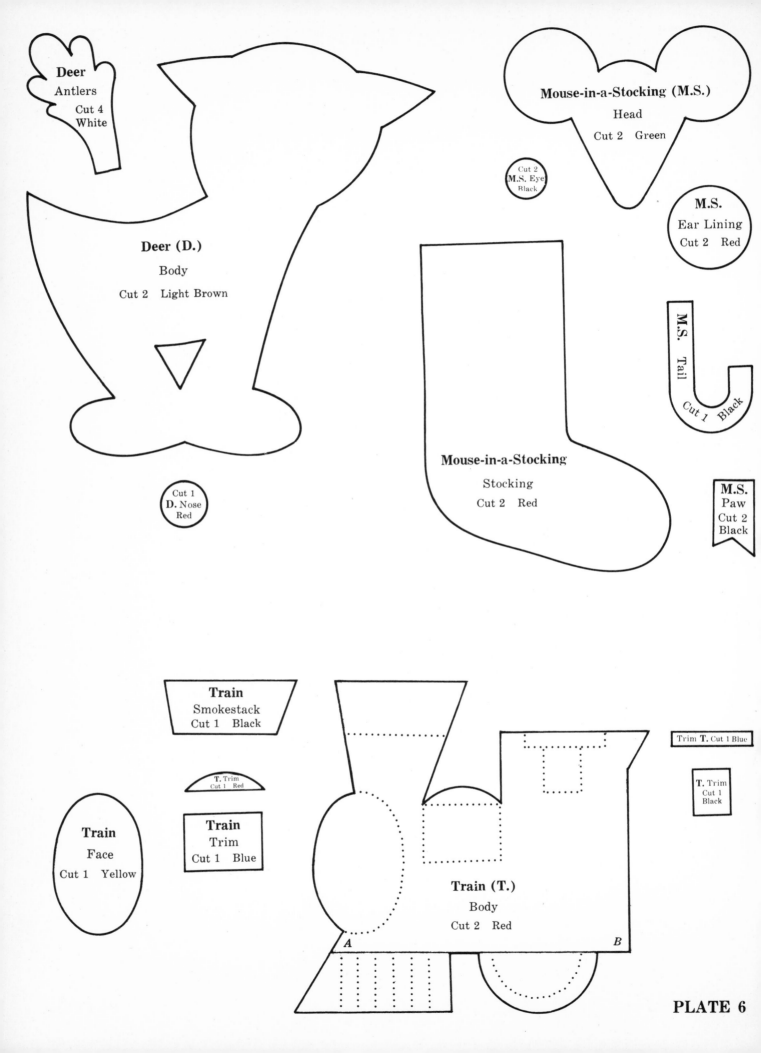

Deer
Antlers
Cut 4
White

Deer (D.)
Body
Cut 2   Light Brown

Cut 1
D. Nose
Red

Mouse-in-a-Stocking (M.S.)
Head
Cut 2   Green

Cut 2
M.S. Eye
Black

M.S.
Ear Lining
Cut 2   Red

M.S.
Tail
Cut 1   Black

M.S.
Paw
Cut 2
Black

Mouse-in-a-Stocking
Stocking
Cut 2   Red

Train
Smokestack
Cut 1   Black

T. Trim
Cut 1   Red

Train
Trim
Cut 1   Blue

Train
Face
Cut 1   Yellow

Trim **T.** Cut 1 Blue

T. Trim
Cut 1
Black

Train (T.)
Body
Cut 2   Red

A

B

PLATE 6

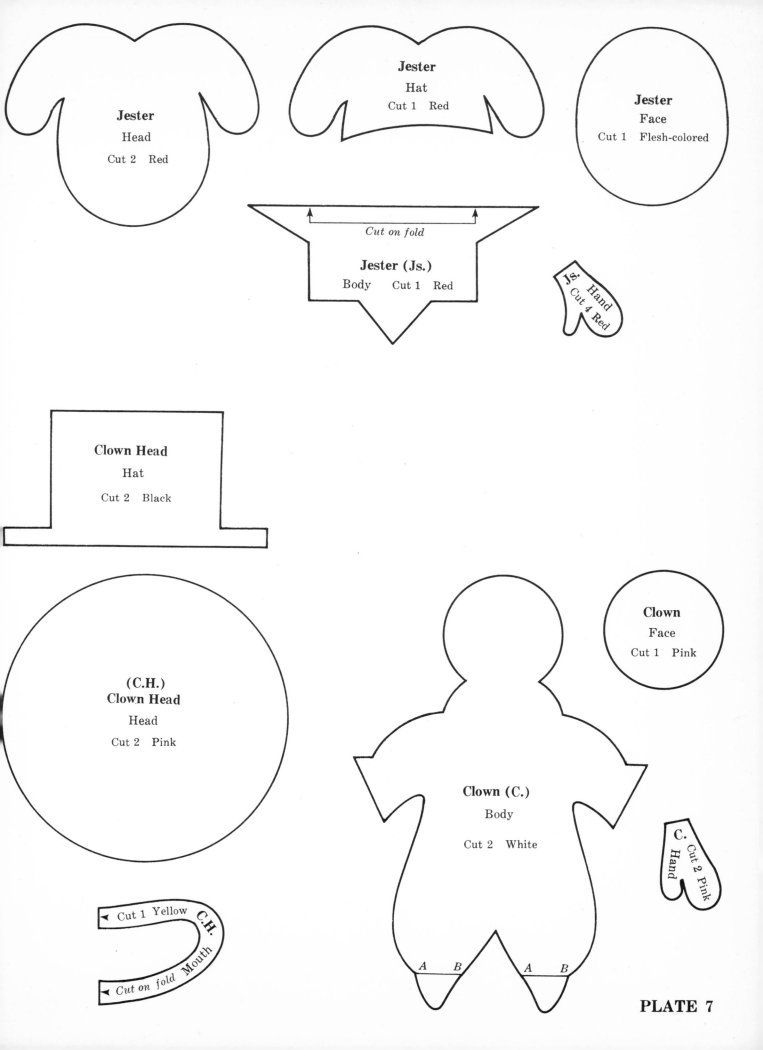

Jester
Head
Cut 2 Red

Jester
Hat
Cut 1 Red

Jester
Face
Cut 1 Flesh-colored

Cut on fold

Jester (Js.)
Body   Cut 1 Red

Js. Hand
Cut 4 Red

Clown Head
Hat
Cut 2   Black

(C.H.)
Clown Head
Head
Cut 2   Pink

Clown
Face
Cut 1   Pink

Clown (C.)
Body
Cut 2   White

C. Cut 2 Pink
Hand

◄ Cut 1 Yellow   C.H.

◄ *Cut on fold* Mouth

A   B   A   B

PLATE 7

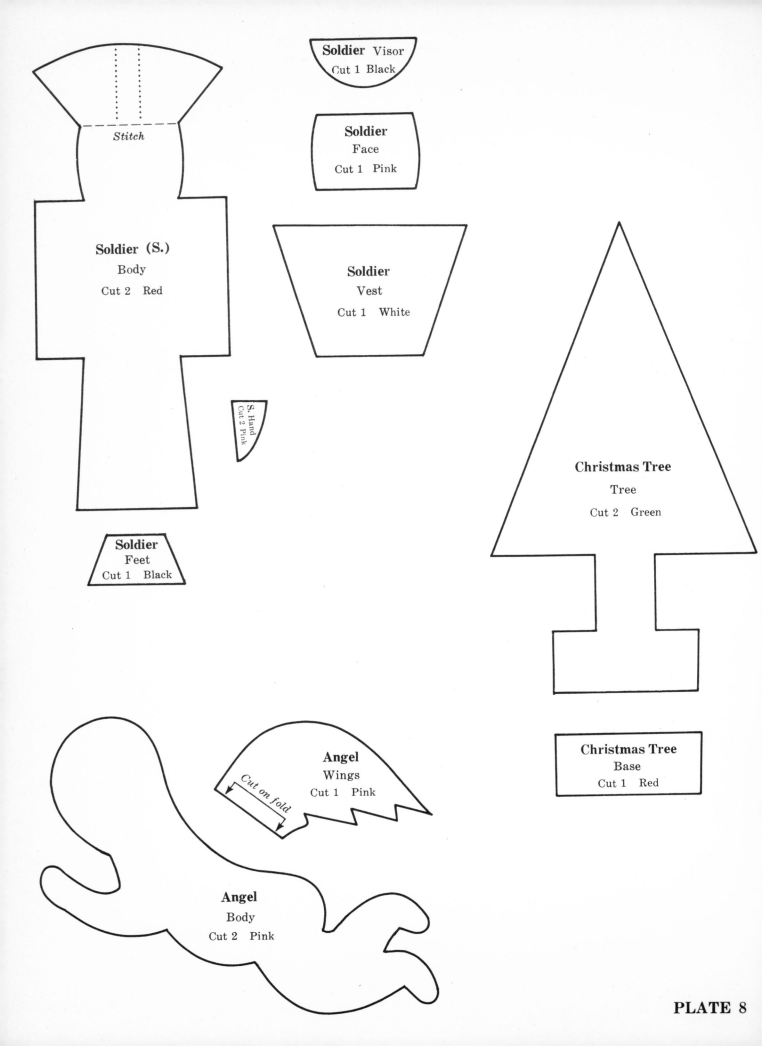

Soldier Visor
Cut 1 Black

Soldier
Face
Cut 1 Pink

Stitch

Soldier (S.)
Body
Cut 2 Red

Soldier
Vest
Cut 1 White

S. Hand
Cut 2 Pink

Soldier
Feet
Cut 1 Black

Christmas Tree
Tree
Cut 2 Green

Angel
Wings
Cut 1 Pink

Cut on fold

Christmas Tree
Base
Cut 1 Red

Angel
Body
Cut 2 Pink

PLATE 8

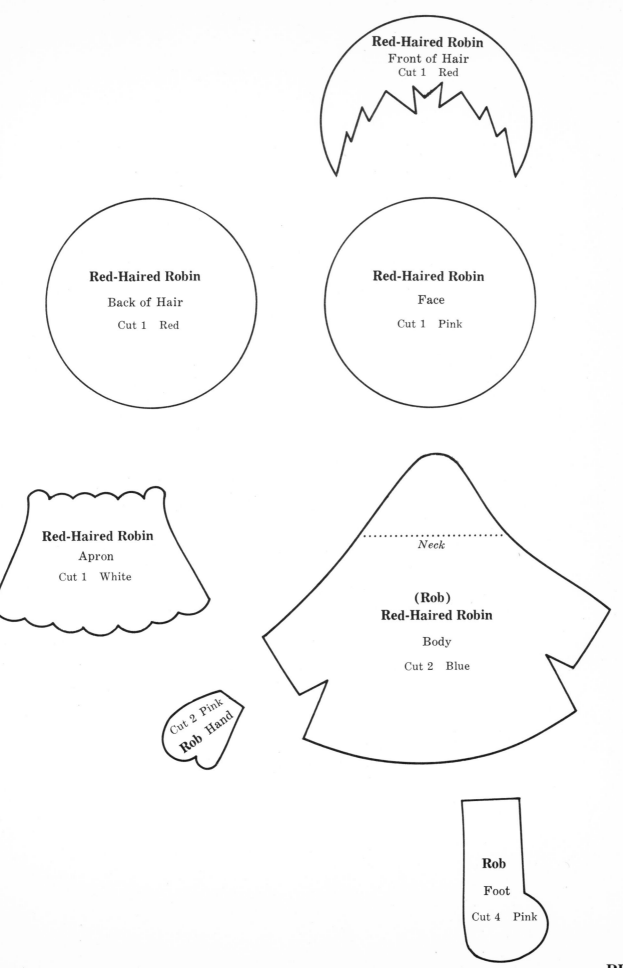

Red-Haired Robin

Front of Hair

Cut 1 Red

Red-Haired Robin

Back of Hair

Cut 1 Red

Red-Haired Robin

Face

Cut 1 Pink

Red-Haired Robin

Apron

Cut 1 White

Neck

(Rob)
Red-Haired Robin

Body

Cut 2 Blue

Cut 2 Pink
Rob Hand

Rob

Foot

Cut 4 Pink

PLATE 9

Red-Haired Roy

Back of Hair

Cut 1   Red

Red-Haired Roy

Front of Hair

Cut 1   Red

Red-Haired Roy

Face

Cut 1   Pink

Red-Haired Roy

Overalls

Cut 2   Blue

Neck

(Roy)
Red-Haired Roy

Body

Cut 2   White

Roy   Hand

Cut 2 Pink

Roy

Foot

Cut 4 Pink

PLATE 10

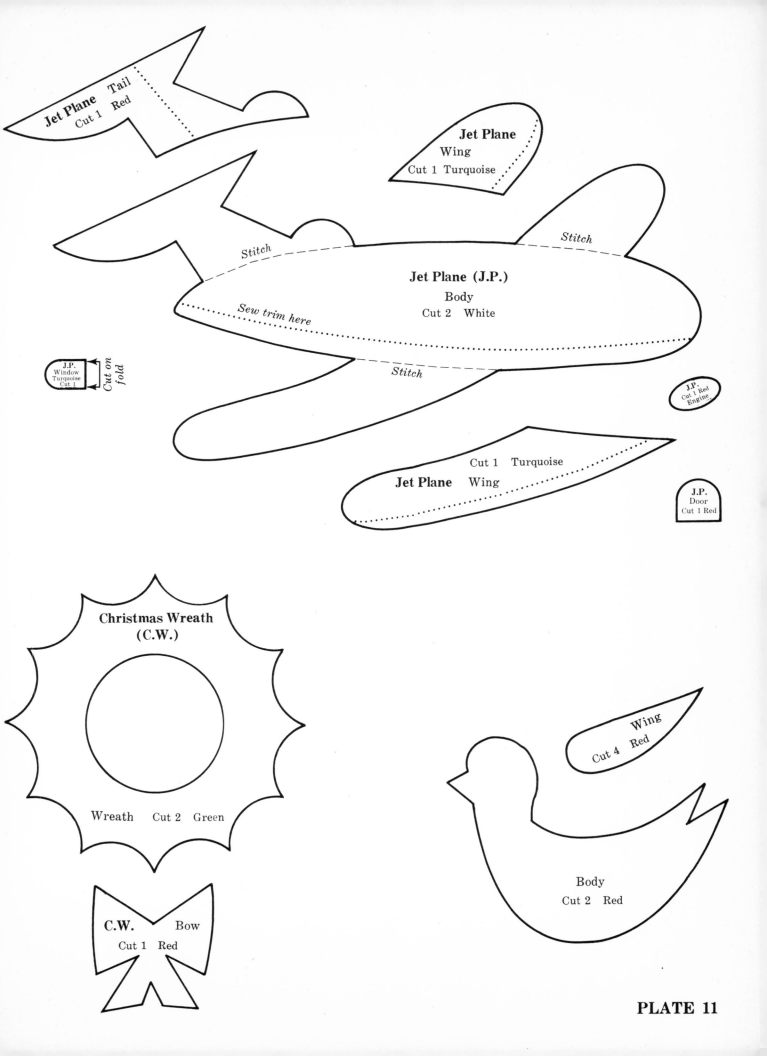

Jet Plane Tail
Cut 1 Red

Jet Plane
Wing
Cut 1 Turquoise

Stitch

Stitch

Jet Plane (J.P.)
Body
Cut 2 White

Sew trim here

Stitch

J.P.
Window
Turquoise
Cut 1

Cut on fold

J.P.
Cut 1 Red
Engine

Cut 1 Turquoise

Jet Plane Wing

J.P.
Door
Cut 1 Red

**Christmas Wreath
(C.W.)**

Wreath Cut 2 Green

C.W. Bow
Cut 1 Red

Wing
Cut 4 Red

Body
Cut 2 Red

PLATE 11

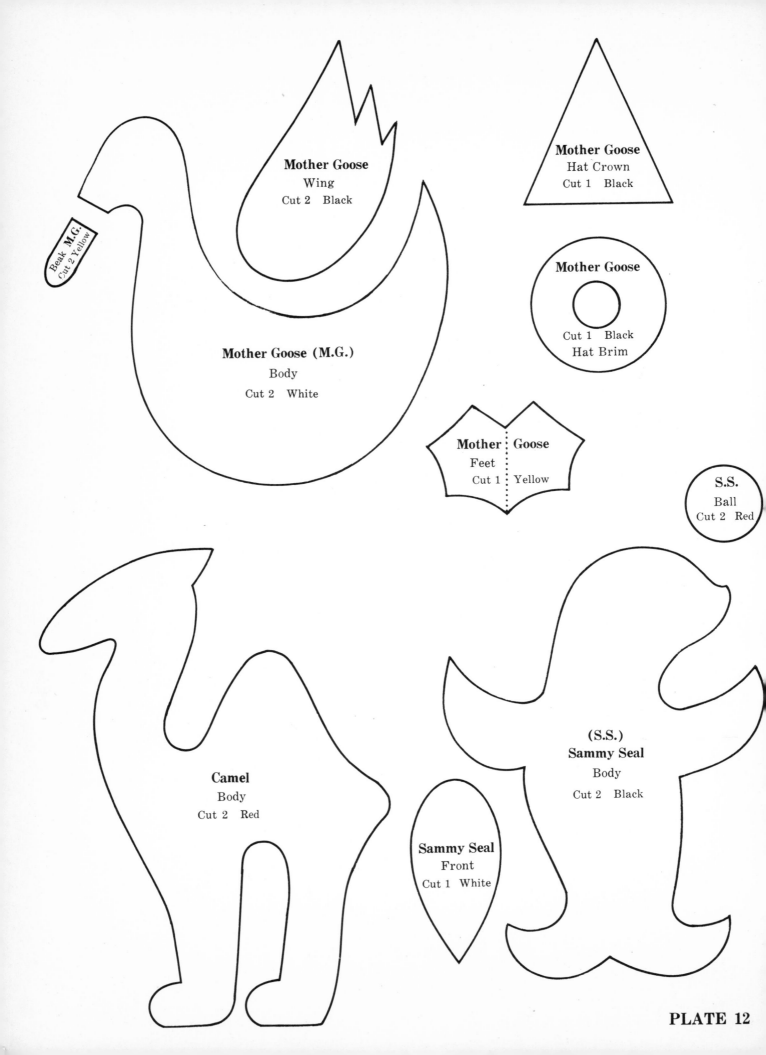

Mother Goose
Wing
Cut 2   Black

Mother Goose
Hat Crown
Cut 1   Black

Beak **M.G.**
Cut 2 Yellow

Mother Goose

Cut 1   Black
Hat Brim

Mother Goose (M.G.)
Body
Cut 2   White

Mother Goose
Feet
Cut 1   Yellow

S.S.
Ball
Cut 2   Red

Camel
Body
Cut 2   Red

(S.S.)
Sammy Seal
Body
Cut 2   Black

Sammy Seal
Front
Cut 1   White

PLATE 12

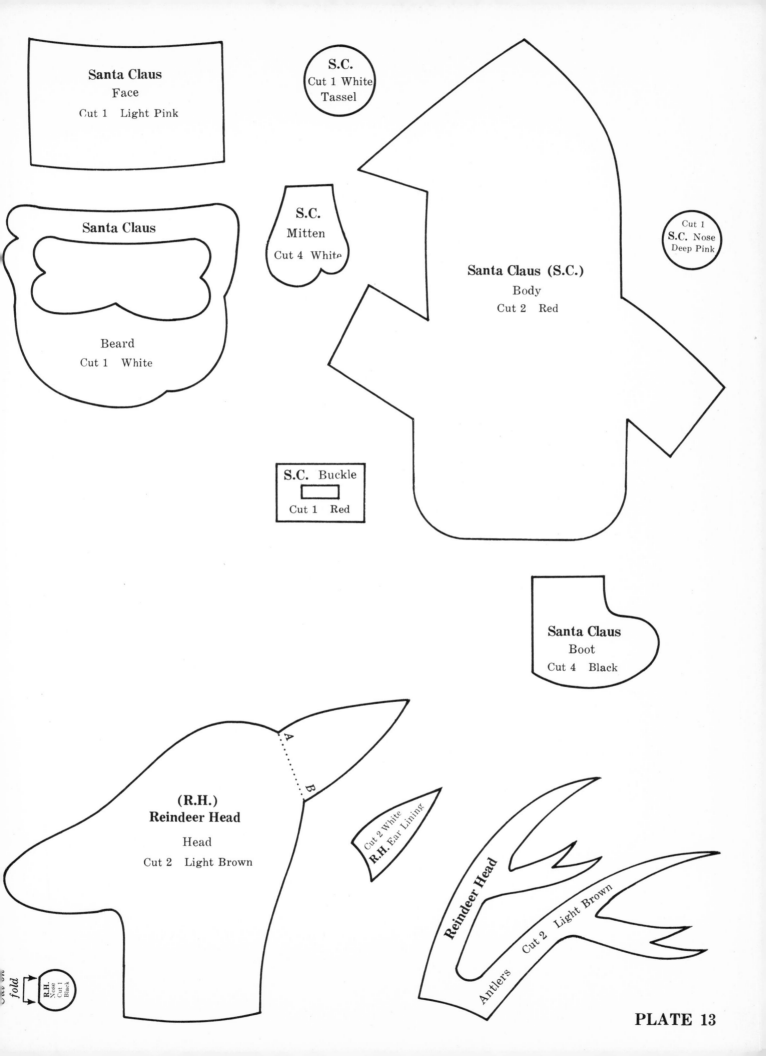

Santa Claus
Face
Cut 1 Light Pink

S.C.
Cut 1 White
Tassel

Santa Claus

Beard
Cut 1 White

S.C.
Mitten
Cut 4 White

Cut 1
S.C. Nose
Deep Pink

Santa Claus (S.C.)
Body
Cut 2 Red

S.C. Buckle
Cut 1 Red

Santa Claus
Boot
Cut 4 Black

A

B

**(R.H.)
Reindeer Head**

Head

Cut 2 Light Brown

Cut 2 White
R.H. Ear Lining

Reindeer Head

Antlers Cut 2 Light Brown

Cut on
fold

R.H.
Nose
Cut 1
Black

PLATE 13

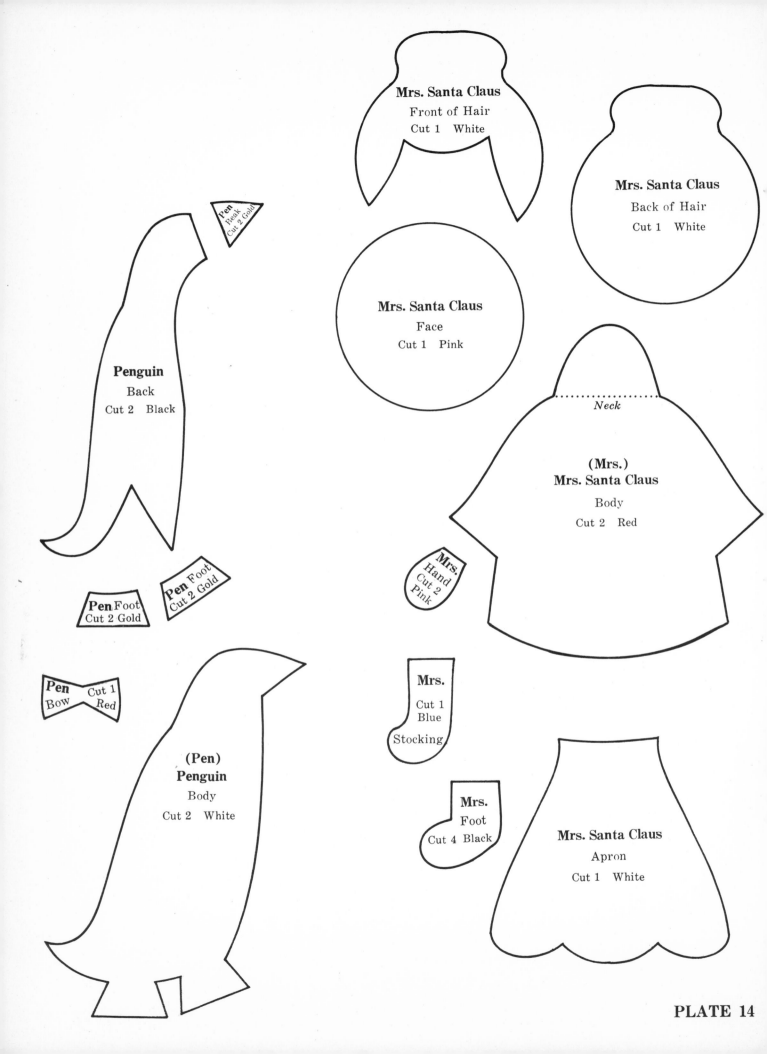

Pen Beak Cut 2 Gold

Penguin
Back
Cut 2   Black

Pen Foot
Cut 2 Gold

Pen Foot
Cut 2 Gold

Pen
Bow   Cut 1
Red

(Pen)
Penguin
Body
Cut 2   White

Mrs. Santa Claus
Front of Hair
Cut 1   White

Mrs. Santa Claus
Back of Hair
Cut 1   White

Mrs. Santa Claus
Face
Cut 1   Pink

Neck

(Mrs.)
Mrs. Santa Claus
Body
Cut 2   Red

Mrs.
Hand
Cut 2
Pink

Mrs.
Cut 1
Blue
Stocking

Mrs.
Foot
Cut 4   Black

Mrs. Santa Claus
Apron
Cut 1   White

PLATE 14

Susie Noël
Front of Hair
Cut 1   Yellow

Susie Noël
Back of Hair
Cut 1   Yellow

Susie Noël
Face
Cut 1   Light Pink

S.N.
Braid
Cut 2
Yellow

(S.N.)
Susie Noël
Body
Cut 2   Red

Susie Noël
Collar   Cut 1
                White

S.N.
Hand
Cut 2
Pink

Susie Noël
Wreath
Cut 1   Green

S.N.
Foot
Cut 2
Pink

Susie Noël
Sleeve
Cut 1   Red

PLATE 15

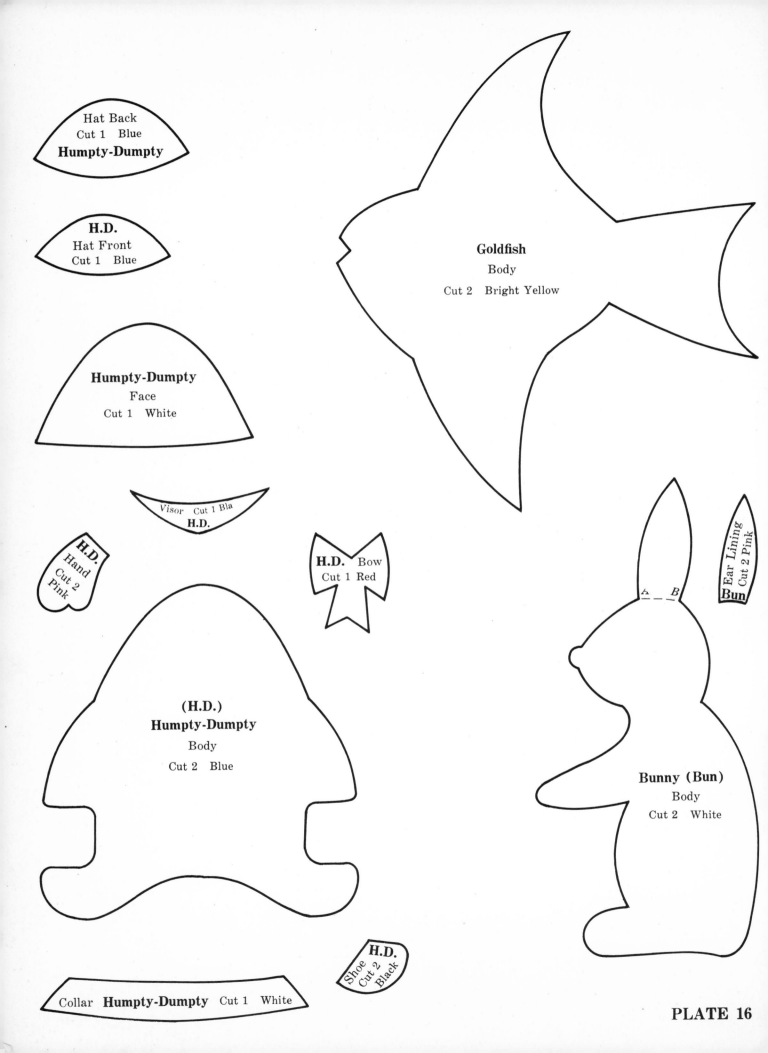

Hat Back
Cut 1   Blue
Humpty-Dumpty

H.D.
Hat Front
Cut 1   Blue

Humpty-Dumpty
Face
Cut 1   White

Visor   Cut 1 Bla
H.D.

H.D.
Hand
Cut 2
Pink

H.D.   Bow
Cut 1 Red

(H.D.)
Humpty-Dumpty
Body
Cut 2   Blue

Goldfish
Body
Cut 2   Bright Yellow

Ear Lining
Cut 2 Pink
Bun

A   B

Bunny (Bun)
Body
Cut 2   White

H.D.
Shoe
Cut 2
Black

Collar   **Humpty-Dumpty**   Cut 1   White

PLATE 16

Susie Noël

The templates used to make this ornament appear on Plate 15.

MATERIALS

Red, yellow, green, white, light pink,
   deep pink and blue felt
Red thread

DIRECTIONS

1. Trace appropriate templates on felt and cut out the pieces.
2. Sew or glue the feet between the two body pieces, following the illustration for placement.
3. Sew the body pieces together, stuffing as you sew.
4. Glue the braids on the back of the face, following the illustration for placement. Let dry, and position face on head so chin is in proper place. Glue face on head.
5. Glue back of hair on the back of the head, and glue front of hair in proper position on the front of the head.
6. Glue white collar and wreath on front, and glue hands on wreath as shown in illustration
7. Position sleeve piece by wrapping around the body. Glue ends of sleeves down on hands, and glue sleeve piece at center back.
8. Cut a strip of white felt with a pinking shears for the trim on the bottom of the gown, and glue on. Decorate wreath with berries made from red felt circles.
9. Glue deep pink circles on the face for cheeks and blue felt circles for eyes. Eyes can also be made with French knots.

Red-Haired Roy

The templates used to make this ornament appear on Plate 10.

MATERIALS

White, blue, pink, red and green felt
White and blue thread

DIRECTIONS

1. Trace appropriate templates on felt and cut out the pieces.
2. Sew hands between the two body pieces. Glue two foot pieces together to make each foot, and sew the feet between the two body pieces.
3. Sew the two body pieces together, stuffing as you sew, but do not stuff the neck.
4. Place the overall pieces on the body, and sew on with overcast stitches from the underarms down the sides and between the legs. Glue down the tops of the overalls.
5. Glue the neck between the face and the back of the hair. Let dry, and glue the front of the hair on the face.
6. Glue blue felt eyes, red felt nose and mouth on the face.
7. Cut out a red felt heart and two green leaves and glue on leg, as shown.

Red-Haired Robin

The templates used to make this ornament appear on Plate 9.

MATERIALS

Blue, red, pink, white and green felt
Blue thread
2 Plastic eyes

DIRECTIONS

1. Trace appropriate templates on felt and cut out the pieces.
2. Sew hands between the two body pieces. Glue two leg pieces together to make each leg, and sew the legs between the two body pieces.
3. Sew the two body pieces together, stuffing as you sew, but do not stuff the neck.
4. Glue the neck between the face and the back of the hair. Let dry, and glue front of hair on face.
5. Glue eyes, red felt nose and mouth on the face.
6. Cut out a red felt heart and two green leaves and glue on apron, as shown. Glue apron on the front of the body.

Penguin

The templates used to make this ornament appear on Plate 14.

MATERIALS

Black, white, gold and red felt
White and black thread
2 Green "jewels"
Flower

DIRECTIONS

1. Trace the appropriate templates on felt and cut out the pieces.
2. Starting with feet and tail, sew together the two body pieces, stuffing as you sew.
3. Fit back pieces on back of the penguin, and stitch down along the back of the penguin. Stitch or glue the rest of the back pieces in place.
4. Glue on beaks, feet, bow, flowers and green "jewels" for eyes.

Camel

The template used to make this ornament appears on Plate 12.

MATERIALS

Red, dark green and light green felt
Red thread
2 Green "jewel" eyes
6 Colored "jewels" (or sequins)
Black embroidery thread (or yarn)

DIRECTIONS

1. Trace the appropriate template on felt and cut out the pieces.
2. Sew strands of black embroidery thread (or yarn) between the two body pieces for the tail and for the tuft on the head. Trim into shape as in illustration.
3. Starting with the legs, sew together body pieces, stuffing as you sew.
4. Cut a strip of dark green felt and sew around the hump. Cut a narrower strip of light green felt and sew on top of the dark green strip.
5. Glue on green "jewel" eyes and colored "jewels" around hump.

Gussie Goose

The templates used to make this ornament appear on Plate 3.

MATERIALS

White, blue, yellow and red felt
White thread
Gold single loop braid
Gold narrow braid
3 Small sequins
Small plastic eye

DIRECTIONS

1. Trace appropriate templates on felt and cut out the pieces.
2. Glue two foot pieces together to make each foot and sew feet between the two body pieces.
3. Sew the two body pieces together, stuffing as you sew.
4. Cut a piece of yellow felt and glue on beak as indicated.
5. Sew hat back to back of head and hat front to front of head. Glue a strip of narrow braid and a piece of single loop braid to hat.
6. Sew front and back pieces of purse together, putting a little stuffing inside the purse.
7. Sew wing to body, sewing or gluing the purse underneath the wing at the same time. Glue single loop braid around the edge of the wing and two sequins on purse.
8. Glue bow on neck, and glue sequin on bow. Glue on eye.

21

Fishing Boy

The templates used to make this ornament appear on Plate 1.

MATERIALS

Red, white, yellow, tan and pink felt
Red and white thread
Yellow burlap
4" Thin stick
4" String or crochet thread
Gold cord

DIRECTIONS

1. Trace appropriate templates on felt and burlap and cut out the pieces.
2. Glue two shoe pieces together and sew between the two body pieces at the bottom center.
3. Sew the two body pieces together, stuffing as you sew.
4. Sew and stuff two arm pieces together, sewing hand in at same time. Repeat for the other arm, and sew both arms to the body at the shoulders.
5. Glue one piece of hat on each side of head, gluing at edges along top and sides. Glue cord around hat.
6. Glue two fish together with one end of the thread between. Wrap and tie the other end of the thread to the stick, placing a little glue over the wrapped thread to hold.
7. Glue the stick between the hands, and attach the other end of the stick to the hat by putting a dab of glue on the side of the hat where the stick touches.
8. Glue pocket and slingshot on hip.

Jenny

The templates used to make this ornament appear on Plate 1.

MATERIALS

Red, white, pink and tan felt
Red and white thread
¼" Twill tape
1½" White eyelet ruffled trim
Flowers
Gold cord

DIRECTIONS

1. Trace appropriate templates on felt and cut out the pieces.
2. Glue two shoes together and sew between the two body pieces at the bottom center.
3. Leaving the brim of the hat loose by stitching from A to B, sew the two body pieces together, stuffing as you sew.
4. Sew and stuff two of the arm pieces together, sewing in the hand at the same time. Repeat for the other arm, and sew both arms to the body at the shoulders.
5. To make the apron, cut a piece of eyelet trim approximately 3½" long, and thread tape through the holes. Put apron on the girl, and tie the tape in a bow.
6. Glue cord around hat.
7. Put flowers between hands and glue hands together.

Christmas Tree

The templates used to make this ornament appear on Plate 8.

MATERIALS

Green and red felt
Green and red thread
Gold sunburst sequin
10 "Jewels"
Gold cord

DIRECTIONS

1. Trace appropriate templates on felt and cut out the pieces.
2. Sew two tree pieces together, stuffing as you sew.
3. Sew red base over base of tree, and decorate with "jewels," gold cord and sunburst sequin.

Old-Fashioned Boot

The templates used to make this ornament appear on Plate 4.

MATERIALS

Red and green felt
Red and green thread
Gold double loop braid
Gold narrow braid
8 Small red sequins
8 Tiny pearls
Red yarn bow

DIRECTIONS

1. Trace appropriate templates on felt and cut out the pieces.
2. Sew the two boot pieces together, stuffing as you sew.
3. Sew trim on boot along line indicated on the template.
4. Glue double loop braid along the edge of the trim and narrow braid along heel.
5. Glue red sequins on trim, and glue pearls on the center of each sequin.
6. Sew red yarn bow on boot.

Train

The templates used to make this ornament appear on Plate 6.

MATERIALS

Red, yellow, blue and black felt
Red and yellow thread
Gold double loop braid
2 Plastic eyes
Red sunburst sequin
Small red sequin
Large red sequin
Large green sequin

DIRECTIONS

1. Trace appropriate templates on felt and cut out pieces.
2. On one body, cut from A to B and discard the bottom piece. Sew the two body pieces, stuffing as you sew, and close at the bottom (A to B).
3. On the bottom of the complete body, glue black strips of felt and a black half circle in place where indicated. Glue half of red sunburst sequin on the half circle, and glue a strip of braid from A to B.
4. Sew face on front. Glue on two plastic eyes and red sequin nose, and draw a mouth with red ink.
5. Glue smokestack and other decorations in place where indicated.
6. Glue a strip of gold braid at edge of smokestack, a large red sequin on the blue square and half of the large green sequin on the black square.

Soldier

The templates used to make this ornament appear on Plate 8.

MATERIALS

Red, black, pink and white felt
Red and pink thread
Gold double loop braid
Gold single loop braid
7 Gold sequins
1 Red sequin
2 Plastic eyes

DIRECTIONS

1. Trace appropriate templates on felt and cut out the pieces.
2. Sew black feet and pink hands between body pieces, and sew face on body front.
3. Begin sewing and stuffing body piece pieces together at the hat. Sew and stuff the remainder of the ornament. Stuff hat and sew across as indicated.
4. Glue a strip of double loop braid down the center of the pants, and glue the white vest in position following the illustration. Glue six gold sequins on the vest.
5. Sew black visor across bottom of hat, leaving free at bottom curve, and glue a strip of white felt and a gold sequin on hat. Glue single loop braid on shoulders and sleeve cuffs.
6. Glue on red sequin nose and 2 plastic eyes.

Jack-in-the-Box

The templates used to make this ornament appear on Plate 4.

MATERIALS

Red, pink and white felt
Red and pink thread
Gold single loop braid
Gold narrow braid
6 Small gold sequins
1 Small red sequin
2 Large red sequins
1 Red "jewel"
1 Green sunburst sequin
2 Plastic eyes

DIRECTIONS

1. Trace appropriate templates on felt and cut out the pieces.
2. Sew or glue hands behind edges of sleeves of body front, and glue or sew hat to body front where indicated.
3. Sew body front to body back and box front to body back, stuffing as you sew.
4. Glue the hat trim on the bottom of the hat, a strip of single loop braid above the trim, three small gold sequins above the braid and three small gold sequins on the tips of the hat.
5. Glue narrow braid along sleeves and down the center of the front.
   Glue a large red sequin on the braid on the front.
6. Glue the collar on the shoulders, and glue single loop braid along the center of the collar.
7. Glue single loop braid, with the loops pointing inside, to the four sides of the box and glue the circular box trim in the center of the box.
   Glue the sunburst sequin and the "jewel" in the center of the box trim.
8. Glue on eyes, small red sequin for nose and half of large sequin for mouth.

Clown

The templates used to make this ornament appear on Plate 7.

MATERIALS

White, red and pink felt
White and pink thread
Orange rug yarn
2 Plastic eyes
Gold double loop braid
4 Colored "jewels"
4 Gold stars
1 Red sequin
1 Green spangle sequin

DIRECTIONS

1. Trace appropriate templates on felt and cut out the pieces.
2. From one body piece, cut off the feet from A to B. (This piece now becomes the front.) Using a pinking shears, cut two thin strips of red felt the length of A to B. Sew these strips in back of the body front at points A to B, allowing the felt to show as a ruffle.
3. Sew hands between two body pieces, and sew the body pieces together, stuffing as you sew.
4. Sew face piece on front.
5. Glue double loop braid along sleeves and down the front of the clown. Cut an oblong of red felt, approximately 1" x 1½", with pinking shears and glue on neck.
6. To make hair, glue pieces of orange rug yarn to head as illustrated. Glue on eyes, red sequin nose and tears cut from green spangle sequins. Glue stars on ruffle, and jewels on braid.
7. Draw mouth with red ink.

Lamb

The templates used to make this ornament appear on Plate 5.

MATERIALS

White, black and red felt
White thread
Red worsted yarn
Flat flowers

DIRECTIONS

1. Trace appropriate templates on felt and cut out the pieces.
2. Sew face piece to body front, leaving the lower part free from A to B.
3. Glue ear linings to ears.
4. Beginning with legs, sew body pieces together, sewing ears between body pieces, and stuffing as you sew.
5. For yarn hair, loop yarn around three fingers 14 times; tie in center and cut ends. Fan out the ends and sew at knot to front of head, trimming ends as in illustration. Repeat this procedure for the hair on the back of the head.
6. Glue on black felt nose and eyelashes, and flowers under the chin.

Mother Goose

The templates used to make this ornament appear on Plate 12.

MATERIALS

White, black and yellow felt
White and black thread
Red worsted yarn or ribbon
2 Blue "jewels"
4 Flat red flowers

DIRECTIONS

1. Trace appropriate templates on felt and cut out the pieces.
2. Fold edges of one beak over the other and stitch in between body
   pieces at mouth.
3. Starting at mouth, sew body pieces together, stuffing as you sew.
4. Stitch feet to bottom with point at center front, and sew wings on body,
   following illustration.
5. Glue blue "jewel" eyes on each side of head.
6. Put red yarn (or ribbon) around head and tie in bow. Fit brim of hat
   down over head, stretching to fit, and sew to head with a few stitches.
   Roll crown piece into a cone; stitch down one side, stuffing as you sew.
   Sew on brim.
7. Glue flowers around crown of hat.

Humpty-Dumpty

The templates used to make this ornament appear on Plate 16.

MATERIALS

Blue, white, red, pink and black felt
Blue and white thread
1 Large red sequin
1 Gold sequin
Gold double loop braid
Gold single loop braid
2 Plastic eyes

DIRECTIONS

1. Trace appropriate templates on felt and cut out the pieces.
2. Sew hands between the two body pieces, and sew the body pieces together, stuffing as you sew.
3. Sew face on body.
4. Sew visor under front hat piece and stitch front hat piece to head. Sew back hat piece to back of head.
5. Glue while collar across the front of the body, and glue double loop braid on the collar and the red bow and a gold sequin on the braid.
6. Glue shoes on each foot, and glue a piece of single loop braid on each sleeve.
7. Glue a red sequin nose, a piece of the large red sequin cut in the shape of a mouth and two plastic eyes on the face.

Jet Plane

The templates used to make this ornament appear on Plate 11.

MATERIALS

White, red and turquoise felt
White thread
Gold narrow flat braid
11 Turquoise sequins
1 Large red sequin
1 Small red sequin

DIRECTIONS

1. Trace appropriate templates on felt and cut out the pieces.
2. Sew two body pieces together, stuffing as you sew, leaving wings and tail free by sewing across as indicated.
3. Glue the two pieces of each wing and tail together. Glue the red tail over the front of the white tail and the turquoise wings over the front of the white wings.
4. Glue braid on the edges of the wings, on the tail and across the length of the body.
5. Glue window on front, placing the fold on the front seam. Glue on red door and red engine as in illustration.
6. Glue on turquoise sequins for windows. Glue small red sequin on engine and large red sequin on tail.